Silver Raindrops In My Eye

Silver Raindrops In My Eye

Bereavement, Loss, Hope and Healing

Poems by

Wild Woman

Edited by AnnMarie Reynolds

for

begin a book Writing Services & Independent Publishers

Copyright © 2024 by Wild Woman

All rights reserved.

No portion of this book may be reproduced in any form without written permission from the publisher or author, except as permitted by United Kingdom copyright law.

This publication is designed to provide accurate and authoritative information in regard to the subject matter covered. It is sold with the understanding that neither the author nor the publisher is engaged in rendering legal, investment, accounting, medical or other professional services.

While the publisher and author have used their best efforts in preparing this book, they make no representations or warranties with respect to the accuracy or completeness of the contents of this book and specifically disclaim any implied warranties or merchantability or fitness for a particular purpose. No warranty may be created or extended by sales representatives or written sales materials.

Neither the publisher nor the author shall be liable for any loss of profit or any other commercial damages, including, but not limited to, special, incidental, consequential, personal, or other damages.

Book Cover by AnnMarie Reynolds (some elements AI generated)

First paperback edition published in the United Kingdom in 2024

ISBN (Print) 978-1-915353-24-5
ISBN (eBook) 978-1-915353-25-2

Published by *begin a book Independent Publishers*

www.beginabook.com

Additional Books by Wild Woman (available on Amazon):

Harvest Time - A Bumper Crop of Poems

Harvest Time is a book brimming with delightful insight as seen through the eyes of Wild Woman. Her vividly striking poems capture the sweet harmony and essence of nostalgia and her passion for the countryside radiates throughout.

Treat yourself to a cuppa, curl up and enjoy this beautifully written anthology of poems.

ISBN: 978-1-915353-00-9

Still Glides the Stream, Fast Flows the River - Short Stories

Still Glides the Stream is a delightfully different collection of tales moving swiftly from story to story with warmth and charm. Wild Woman has a profoundly entertaining gift of creating irresistible characters you feel you know, and would like to stay with much longer.

Exploring her versatility becomes an unusual and entertaining experience when she portrays situations in an unconventional and thought-provoking way.

She is delighted to share her fresh and colourful array of stories with you today.

ISBN: 978-1-915353-03-0

The secret life of Wild Woman remains mysteriously quiet on information...

*Somewhere there is a bright and beautiful garden,
Where tears flow freely,
And the sound of weeping
Rustles the leaves on the trees.
Sunlight warms the despairing heart
And love finds a way through the woods,
When all the while the sky above
Is a hazy, translucent blue.*

Any loss can leave you breathless. Wild Woman hopes that her poems will help to lighten your darkness and give birth to hope and fresh, brighter days ahead.

Contents

Silver Raindrops in my Eye	13
Tick Tock	14
Oh, Precious Love	15
Love. Life. Loss.	16
Riding the Waves	17
What Should I Do?	18
Time Flies	20
Sailing By	22
Dramatic Morning	23
Music	24
Angels and Rainbows	25
Soon	26
White Feather	27
The Goose	28
Maurice The Wood Mouse	30
Chocolate	31
The Sunflower Lifted Its Big Head and Smiled	32
At Night	34
Speed	35
Part of the Family	36
Now You Are Gone	37
A Lady in a Fog	38
Secrets	39
Spiritual Wisdom	40
Samson	41
New Day	42
How Long?	43
Get a Tonic from the Forest	44
Three Years Ago	46
Starry Night	47
A Healing Weather Forecast	48
Thoughts	49
Autumn Leaves	50
Golden Fingered Dawn	51

Give it Time	52
Bright Sunlight	53
More Rain	54
Echoes of a Lost Voice	55
Memories	56
What Next?	57
Pink Clouds	58
Low Ebb	59
Footsteps in the Snow	60
Bothered	61
Sweet Earth	62
The Phone	63
Lost	64
Another Day Dawning	65
The Greedy Sea	66
I Spy with My Little Eye	68
Miles Away	69
Little White Feather	70
Take Time	71
A Prayer	72
Night-time Treasure in the Heavens	73
Beauty and Wonder of the Spirit	74
Helping Hand	75
Soulmate	76
Pending	77
I Love You Long and Dearly	78
What time is it?	79
Silver Chain	80
A Murmuration of Starlings	81
Pursue Tomorrow	82
The Essence of the Sea	83
I Wept (for my child)	87
Miscarriage	88
Teardrops (for my child)	89
To the Abused, Bereaved	90
Beyond Grief	92
The Swans (a traumatic death)	94

Silver Raindrops in my Eye

Walk with me, talk with me,
I don't want to cry.
Silver raindrops in my eye.

Don't let the day go by
Without thought of you by my side.
Silver raindrops in my eye.

Not as you left all shrivelled up and depressed,
But as the golden rain fell upon your head,
We did not care for we were a pair,
Huddled together under an umbrella.
Silver raindrops in my eye.

We thought we were together, forever,
Whatever the weather.
Silver raindrops in my eye.

We talked to each other,
A sign of our strength,
But what now is left?
Memories; and silver raindrops in my eye.

When we first met, he said,
"How many children will we have?"
When he left, he said, "Goodbye."
So many things we did.
And all I can do now is sigh and cry.
Silver raindrops in my eye.

Tick Tock

The clock ticked too loud.
It ticked off the hours.
Time to get up, time for bed,
Tick tock, tick tock.
Time just flew by, no time to say goodbye.
It was relentless; it would not stop.
Days led to years.
Tick tock, tick tock.
Dreams were there only to perish the next day,
How could life tick-tock away?
Snow, wind and rain never seemed to stay.
So, how can love perish in a similar way?
Tick tock, tick tock.
How could time whisk you away?
Where did you go?
I fail to see why you and I had to part.
And the clock tick-tocked away.
Strongly and audibly, it just tick-tocked away.

Oh, Precious Love

You were a gift to me, and I a gift to you.
You were in me and I in you.
I said our love would last forever,
Forever is a long time, you said.
Oh, precious love,
Think of us always together,
Whatever the weather,
The time or the place.
Oh, precious love,
You left, I stayed,
But we are still together,
The thread will not be severed.
Oh, precious love,
You are inscribed upon my heart,
I knew that from the start,
We just belong together,
Now we are apart.
The silver thread will keep us tethered,
Forever, and ever and ever.
Oh, precious love,
A rocky, wild and barren land,
Is where I stand,
But you are in a garden,
Near at hand, and you continue looking after me.
Oh, precious love,
And I know that you are near,
And with the gift you gave to me,
I will serve others with that precious love and power.

Love. Life. Loss.

Did I love too much?
Were we too close?
There can never be too much love.

We loved our lives,
The breath of life
Filled our hearts every single day.

Loss.
We never talked of loss.
Something you carry around each day.

Riding the Waves

I say your name every day,
My love.
I thought there was something not quite right,
My love.
For you were cast adrift in a lonely place,
My love.
Fighting for the right to live,
My love.
You battled on from day to day,
My love.
And then you were no more,
My love.
I'm floating in a sea of grief,
My love.
The waves are strong and rough,
My love.
They say that the weather will get better,
My love.
And I look forward to that day,
My love.
When I can say your name,
My love.
Without this terrible hurt,
My love.
Without this terrible hurt.

What Should I Do?

I know to eat the food I should,
The things I hope will do me good.
The greens, the peas and beans,
And the bright red berries.
A drink of tea, that pleases me.
And I go to the keep fit class.

No one told me what grief would be.
Complete misery.
Disturbed and distressed.
So much desolation.
How could anyone feel so much?
Please, no more suffering.

I know they said it would get better,
But how could that possibly be?
Life stolen from me.
You did not intend to desert your family,
And leave us all on our own.
Our children have no idea where you have gone.

What do I say? What do I tell them?
I try so hard to keep it all together.
I'm told that each day should get better,
But your voice and laughter are slipping away.

I study your photo every day,
So, the memory will not fade.

Our lives were happy, not a single thought,
Of losing you.
Please, what should I do?
I had a dream last night,
You told me to hold onto your invisible hand,
And you would not leave me until the end of time.

Time Flies

No time to think, no time to plan,
What I should do when he had gone.
They did not tell me of the pain,
It felt as if I had been slain,
And thoughts rose up to trick my mind,
To tell me that everything was fine.
I jogged down the path of memory lane,
It was no help to keep me sane.
The music in my head did stop,
And my days went downwards, drop by drop.
Until I shook myself awake,
To tell myself this will not do,
To mope about from room to room.
I decided I should get on and move on.
Bit by bit I took my time,
To go on out and meet my friends,
Who were waiting there for me to appear,
So that I could clear the air,
And free myself so I could care,
Once more for the days ahead.
I had changed from the 'Old Me',
To a completely new sort of person,
Who could see more, feel more, understand more,
And who knew what life was for.
We start as a baby, then a tiny tot,
School child, teenager, young person,

Middle-aged, getting older, pensioner,
Then, in our golden years,
We rapidly move on to possibly,
Widower or widow, single parent or guardian.
Change is inevitable,
It's how we grow – mature and understand it all.
And like a bird of the air, we fly through life unprepared.
Uncle, aunt, cousin, mother, father, husband, wife.
So, live each day with intent,
Breathe vitality and lots of energy,
Through life.

Sailing By

Sail along with me,
Stay a little longer.
I know you had to leave,
But please, let's sail once more,
Across the deep blue sea.
Your ashes will ride the crest of a wave,
And sail the oceans every day.
Our jolly boat will float along beside you.
Sea-going days are not over.
We will float along together,
Navigate every lift and plummet of the sea.
Exposed to view to the soaring sea birds,
And the wind and the sky whisper together.
Those happy days remembered forever.

Dramatic Morning

Ice-ringing-bright white dazzling the eye,
The smell of fresh beauty that fell from the sky.
Open air freedom, I sucked it all in.
Why do I feel that I want to cry?
Sunlight, blue sky, the crunch of my feet,
A fizz up my nose and hard muscled belly.
I felt faint with the radiant force
As it took my breath away.
It was deep, frosty, cold,
And my hand stuck to the garden gate.
I drew near, hoping I would not be late.
I put my fingertips to my lips,
To taste ice crystals of rust and dust,
That had accumulated over the years.
My legs were terribly numb
From treading through the winter snow.
My car had slid from side to side,
As it careered over the icy road,
To end up at the kerbside edge,
Wheels deeply embedded in a drift of snow.
A walk of a mile had led me home,
Where the cat and my dog welcomed me back,
As I stamped the snow from off my boots,
And made a fuss of my endearing, affectionate friends,
Who never complained if a meal was late.
Hailstorm, hoar frost and freezing snow,
How could temperatures plunge so low?
And no one complains or despairs,
And summer is shortening to a few warm days.
All I have are my pets to stay by me.
I am lost, but my pets stay beside me every day.

Music

Music flowed through my head,
All jumbled and distorted.
A rumble of thunder,
That tried to unwind,
It was stuck in a twist,
Knotted together wanting to unravel
To make sense of music
I could understand.
The chain of events
Were soul-distressing
But in the New Year,
My sad soul melted,
The music I knew was restored.
I awoke to the sound of
Loving emotion.
Tears were let loose,
And I began to understand
That the music I heard
When I grieved was absurd.
Only later did my mind
Clear to the fear of you not here.
The music I need will enfold,
My mind, and once more,
Will I hear of the wonderful time
We were together.
Music will play once again,
In my mind, over and over,
Until I reclaim my tune
Of you, the one you liked to play.

Angels and Rainbows

(For the young who have lost a member of their family)

Angels flew across my bedroom last night,
I saw them clear and so bright.
They showed me their wings
And their pretty toes and things,
And whispered low and explained,
That the person that I knew had died
Was there on the other side.
Not far away, but being looked after
By other rainbow people.
The angels said that they would
Watch over me and keep me safe,
And to look out for a white feather
That would tell me that all was well
With the one I loved.
And on a wet day when the sun comes out
To look for the rainbow in the sky.
To let me know that all angels can fly
And Robins are special and will remind me
That my dear one is not lost.
No. Simply
Living in a different way,
Not far away.
So, when a snowflake falls to the ground,
Each single crystal will show that
Angels come in different forms
And they still love you every day.

Soon

Thank you for the life you gave me
You set my soul ablaze.
Music of the angels
Filters down from the heavens,
Opened wide to see,
That I was all right.
And let me know that,
We shall hold hands again,
Anon.

White Feather

I found a soft white feather yesterday,
Where did it come from?
I just don't know.
I can't understand it.
It was on my bedroom floor.
They say an angel dropped it,
To say hello,
And to let me know that my loved ones
Were not far away.
And now today another feather,
Lay on the bathroom floor.
I just know it was never there before.
I gathered up my feathers and put them in a drawer.
I had been told it was a loving message,
That had been dropped at my door.

The Goose

I wandered in my country garden by the babbling brook.
I had never felt so alone or heaved so many sighs.
My rescue birds around me, a few hens and some ducks.
I sat down upon a stone; I could not believe how grieved I was.
My hurt, distress and sorrow had been building up for days.
I could not yet get away from my blanket of black haze.
Who was there to hold my hand when I was so dismayed?
I bowed my head to say, 'Please, is there someone to help me through the day?'
I heard a little 'honk', it was coming my way.
It was my forlorn goose who had lost his lifelong mate.
The goose was slowly edging, shuffling my way.
He gave another 'honk' to indicate I should stay.
Seated in my misery I watched him gently sway.
He came right up behind me and opened up his wings,
He held them out to shelter me, I did not move away.
He kept them stretched around me in such a protective way.
Then, 'honk, honk,' he moved to stand in front of me.
His neck was stiff and straight, his eyes aligned with mine,
He came to sympathise with me and drink in all my pain.
He lowered down his silky crown and laid it upon my thigh.
Ethereally, light and airily, I stroked his little head.
He 'honked' again to tell me he knew what I had felt.
Oh my – what a shock that was –
Something else was there instead.
Peace and comfort poured over me, love of a different kind.

What energy that was left in me was lifted up on high.
Whoosh – a sudden and amazing presence hovered overhead.
Pure love, overflowing, a shimmering power on every side.
It was euphoric, tender, a calmness for my life.
I felt that something wonderful was telling me that it would be alright.
My fragile weakness would soon leave me,
And I would grow an inward nature of a more sophisticated mind.

Maurice The Wood Mouse

A little wood mouse sat under a toadstool and laughed.
He looked around at his surroundings with his large, beady eyes,
And scratched one of his big, round ears.
Then cleaned his tail before leaning back on the stalk of a fungi.
He could smell the damp leaves that had dropped to the ground,
They looked like shiny, leather patches all around.
He had feasted on fir cones and left them in heaps,
With their scales neatly gnawed right down.
There had been a few wet days,
And Maurice the wood mouse had wet, soggy feet.
He wanted to dry out basking in the warm sunshine
That filtered through the trees.
A languor overtook him as he fell into the arms of Morpheus,
The sleep God,
Only to be jolted from sleep by the warning cry of a blackbird.
Maurice looked all which ways as his little
heart beat umpteen to the dozen.
Was it the dreaded weasel that was near about?
He had spotted the tell-tale twisted droppings only that morning.
How foolish to take a rest when there was a threat to life.
He slowly left his Penny Bun Shelter and hop-skipped home,
Vowing to be more careful. He really wanted to live longer,
He had avoided the owl, the jay and greedy buzzard,
And the beautiful heron that patrols the brook,
And he knew where the foxes hung out.
But the weasel was an eating machine,
Did they say ten meals a day?
Maurice the wood mouse would have to look out.
And hide in the treetops until,
Mr Weasel moved far, far away.

Chocolate

What will help me in a crisis?
Chocolate.
What will soothe me when I'm lost?
Chocolate.
When I'm speechless from emotion
I rely on a nice chocolate bar.
Where is the brown colour in the rainbow?
The missing comforting ray of light.
Was it left out of the sky for a reason?
So, we would look for it somewhere else?
If the bright colours in the sky give us comfort,
Why can't chocolate do the same?
I place a bit of chocolate in my mouth
And let it reside there to slowly melt
And create a warm, friendly, sweet taste.
That will help me modify the pain I have inside.
Mahogany, mocha, coffee-coloured, brown,
A caramel-flavoured chocolate bar
Of the mouth-watering kind.
Give me chocolate every time.
To help me through my hurt and lift me up.
Dreaming deeper, reaching further, seeking a brand-new path.
And another piece of chocolate for my heart.

The Sunflower Lifted Its Big Head and Smiled

Surprise yourself with a closer look,
See things in a different light.
Even looking at silver letters on the spine of a book.
An ant climbing a blade of grass.
Dust motes dancing in the sunbeams ray
Or notice the iridescent blue hue of a discarded jay's feather.
At the start of the autumn season,
Study the spindle berry fruits
That look like blossom on the tree.
Or hear a skylark, just a small spot way up in the sky.
The wind blowing through a field of wheat,
Bobbing and swaying, wave upon wave,
Ripple upon ripple in the breeze.
Deer in the field feeding on next year's hay,
Or have you heard the current of air weaving and whining
Through the telegraph wires?
The hum strum of a dragonfly's wings
As it dances by the stream.
See dark storm clouds and bright red holly berries,
Green and gold leaves in a heap where the squirrels meet.
The bloom upon a bunch of grapes,
Or bubbly scum at the tumbling sea's edge.
Bright light playing on the bark of a silver birch.
Have you seen the flash of a silverfish, slither along
the bathroom floor.
Watch the dark spores rise from a kicked puff ball,

And laughed as you gather the frozen washing off the line.
Wonder at the pink sky in the early morning dawn,
Or see through those coloured cellophane wrappers.
Everything you looked at is all one hazy shade.
Did you count the green lines on a snowdrop flower,
Or watch a snowflake fade into a drop of water on your hand.
And see a chevron flight of geese with their accompanying chatter.
Bright moss like glass on the side of a tree.
And the sunflower lifted its big head and smiled.

At Night

A hoot of an owl, a bark of a fox,
As the moon's bright glow filtered through the trees,
And a slight night breeze blew on the leaves.
While a family of mice ran among the ferny glade,
And moths came together in the scented air.
The ducks sleeping by the water under the willows.
Deer moved silently for a drink by the pond.
The dark, still water where water lilies grow,
And fish swim silently in the murk below.
Tall grasses swayed to and fro,
The bracken lay low with dew.
While the old oak tree saw it all,
As the roosting birds began to stir,
A slight commotion, a bustle, a flurry,
To end their sleep at the first sight of dawn,
And fly up higher around aromatic trees.
Ready for a sing-song as rabbits come out to play.
Squirrels with the first ray of sunlight bounce about,
A blackbird and a robin sing, as a hedgehog bustles along a track.
There are so many things we never see,
We are hidden indoors and don't venture out
To see the beauty of the night.
But hope that everything is alright.

Speed

Slow to unfold the flower bud swells,
Bright colour peeps from within the bracts.
It lengthens and broadens each morning,
Wind, rain, dew and sun
Summon the bursting petals on,
And essence of rose can fill the air,
Each bloom you compare with
Last years which you thought fair.
With the speed of a few weeks,
The shrub is a riot to inspire.
Summer flowers speed you through the year,
Watch each day disappear.
Plant in your heart blossoms
Of love not of fear.
Forget-me-not, foxglove, freesia,
Blossom, bloom and sprout,
The speed the flowers open out.
Emotional feelings are the same,
Pleasure and contentment
Can be brought on by looking at a flower.

Part of the Family

My pet, my pet, my wonderful pet,
He never strayed from my side.
We walked and played most days,
Part of me, part family.
He talked to me, I understood,
Cuddled up on the settee with me.
Tugged on the bedding to wake me up,
Followed me round wherever I went.
He was part of me, yes, my doggie,
I miss you, my friend.
I think I hear you following me upstairs,
I have you still by my side.
As photos on my phone.

Now You are Gone

We fitted together like a foot in a shoe,
We paddled our canoe, two together.
Over the rapids, we held fast,
As we travelled the river of life.
Now you are gone, and I am so forlorn,
No one said how sad I would be without you.
My eyes are wet all the time.
I can't get the grit out.
Oh, beautiful, shining, crystal light,
I miss you so,
My glorious, entranced, wondrous power.
Oh, my love, please.
Water the mirror of my soul,
And live within me forever more.

A Lady in a Fog

I did not sleep all night,
Even when there was no light.
Then, after some hours,
I sat up with a book,
Had a go with some music,
But the demons would not go away.
I tried not to think; it did not work,
So, ran over in my mind,
All the bad things that had happened that day.
From the letter I'd had that made me so sad,
To the bill, I needed to pay.
The food in the cupboard ran out,
Another day on half pay.
What can I do to get it all right?
Bereavement, environment, mental health,
I'm a lady in a fog.
Drowning in droplets of water.
Restricting my view of the world.
I can't tune into the news,
How can I help others through?
I'm so confused as to what to do.
Feeling so angry and resentful,
Because I can't cope with the loss.
It's pulling me down into the dark,
Marshalling my thoughts will not help,
I can't see a way through.
I change my position in bed,
And know the day ahead,
Will be the same as before.
And I will still be a lady in a fog.

Secrets

Family secrets to be kept forever,
Never spoken about but buttoned up to fester.
No one to tell, no one to listen,
Over the years, the problems never got solved,
They escalated, gathering dust.
Crunched up in the mind.
Lurking about in the deep shadows.
Would it be better to go over what took place?
Let it all out, the crippling memories.
Those things known only to a few.
But now, the ones it involved have at last gone,
The secrets you kept are still there in your head,
How much harm to anyone now?
Could it matter anymore?
A secret no one wants to hear.
But you still want to talk about what you know.
To be released at last, from the things of the past.

Spiritual Wisdom

The darkness began to thin
And the birds began to sing.
Like a leaf from a tree, in the stream,
I just kept bobbing along.
Up and over the pebbles,
Under the bridge,
I sailed on and on.
The sky, the birds, the leaf,
The water, pebbles and a bridge.
I was on my way.
The sky was blue,
The bird song was merry,
The leaf was green,
The water cleansing.
The pebbles were smooth,
The bridge, a gap to go through.
And I more happily sailed on.

Samson

I miss you.
My cat would nap on my lap,
Or cuddle up between my feet.
He liked to curl out in the sun
And climb the fence and chase the birds.
He brought me mice he caught in the night,
And was there to welcome me home at the door.
He told me what he liked to eat,
But best of all he slept with me.
His whiskers tried to tickle me.
His tail would slap me in the face,
And his purr would tell me that he felt safe.
He was my favourite pet.
The first I ever had.
Samson, my cat.

New Day

Give me strength in my legs to keep walking,
Give me strength in my limbs each morning.
Give me strength to keep on talking,
At the beginning of each new day.

Give me strength to cook my food,
Give me strength to clean my rooms.
Give me strength to open a letter,
At the beginning of each new day.

Give me strength to do my garden,
Give me strength to mow the lawn.
Give me strength to pick the veg,
At the beginning of each new day.

Give me strength to go out shopping,
Give me strength to meet my friends.
Give me strength to make a phone call,
At the beginning of each new day.

Give me strength to get a drink,
Give me strength to rest a bit.
Give me strength when I'm all alone,
At the beginning of the long, long day.

Give me strength to take more pills,
Give me strength to eat more food.
Give me strength to climb the stairs for bed,
At the end of a long, lonely day.

How Long?

How long have we got?
Not long enough,
To right the wrongs and help the poor.

How long have we got?
Not long enough,
To save the seas and polluted ponds.

How long have we got?
Not long enough,
To till the ground and sow the seeds.

How long have we got?
Not long enough,
To clean the water, we need to drink.

How long have we got?
Not long enough,
To say sorry and be kind to each other.

Look up, look up from your computer screen.
Look up, look up from the book you read.
Look up, look up from the phone keypad.
Look up, look up and see the world.
Look up, look up, and what do you see?

Beauty, heartache, love, disease,
What difficult experiences have you just received?

How long have we got?

Not long enough,
To stay in tune with the nature of things.

Get a Tonic from the Forest

Experiencing sorrow and grief,
They say these are strong emotions,
That would stay with me a little longer.
Flowing through me are deep, hurtful feelings.
Is there a medicine I can use to relieve the pain?
Can I share my thoughts with others?
And will anyone want to listen?
I fill my days with a lot of work,
All energy has faded away.
Negative thoughts are in my head,
All through the day.
Blocking my ability to see,
How things really are.
I am out of touch with what's going on,
I must weather the storm and rise up from its depths.
I experience the full spectrum of emotions
Of all I have to go through.
I know that life brings its problems,
But sorrow and grief are hard to bear.
Like a flower, I need the rain,
As much as the sun to flourish.
I feel so dead and withered inside,
I have to persuade my brain to cherish my life,
To overcome the barriers of pain and sadness,
Focus on the good and not the bad,
Think of nice things I can do for myself.
Look forward to plans,
Don't fan the flames of my distress.
Create a ripple of kindness,
Think how I can help others.
The hurt won't go away,

Not for a while, anyway.
Ride the waves of discontent,
The river of tears can fill an ocean.
Will the tears ever stop?
In time, I will understand what I should do,
And make plans of what,
And where I should go.
Take those steps down the road,
Towards contentment.
Don't let the thieves of happiness
Steal joy anymore.
Cherish the new day; steady, get ready,
Like Winter into Spring.
Breathe in deeply the early morning air,
To start the day.
Heal, restore and repair any damage,
Guard and protect that special, safe place.
Be healed and rehabilitated once more.
Vulnerable, but feel the ground beneath my feet.
One small step, head in the right direction,
Get nourished by nature,
Or a tonic from the forest.
Endure the desolation no more.
Explore the power of the great outdoors,
And don't be sad anymore.
Do the things that matter,
Focus on happy times and walk on.
Create some meaning in life.
Every day.

Three Years Ago

Three years ago, you left me,
But still, I feel you now.
Hidden from sight but looking on,
Peeping at all I do.
From day to day, I know you care,
How can I manage without your help?
From paying the bills to making the bed,
To cooking my meals at the time I should.
No talk, no laughter without you,
Sad at heart and no more chatter,
Of us doing things together.
Was still a shock to live through.

Starry Night

In the starry dark night sky,
I see so many sparkling lights.
Are you up there shining down on me?
Or do you fly with angel wings?
It is at night I miss you most,
Are you there or are you lost?
With so many stars up there,
I feel that you can't be far away.
The brightest twinkle must be you,
For you were the splendid light for me.
So, all the luminaries up there,
Keep streaming your gleaming love on me.
I know that you are there,
When the cloudy skies appear.

A Healing Weather Forecast

A warning of gales to come,
Thundery at times,
Rain or showers,
Sensitivity overload.
Buffeting winds of change,
Hope is on the way.
Kindness just around the corner,
Bright spells to look forward to.
Prolonged sunshine, and
Dreamy days ahead.

Thoughts

The deer are in the woodland glade
Before the bright daylight fades away.
They will eat the grass and nibble the bark,
Of trees that make a delicious feed.
They will glide off to the denser wood,
To settle down to a night of sleep,
Only to awake at early dawn
To graze once more in the field of corn.
The lazy insects drone on and on,
Birds black as crows,
Swoop low over the herd of deer,
And follow them wherever they go.
There are lots of things we don't know,
That hide away in our hearts today.
So, hug them tight, don't let them get away.

Autumn Leaves

Autumn leaves came sailing down,
Caught in a gust of wind.
The dancing whirl of the shed foliage,
Swished about my head.
Sunlight flashed upon the leaves,
I followed their movements
As they settled at my feet.
The wind picked them up
And scattered them all around,
To the music of a rustle and bustle.
Then ceased their dancing treat.
I kicked the leaves with my feet,
To disturb them once more
As I walked through the Autumn fall.
Leaves, like confetti, gently touched me,
On the shoulders, like fingertips,
Tapping me to say – 'Yes, I'm still with you'
'Whatever the weather, I am in the leaves'.
The golden array of Nature's display.

Golden Fingered Dawn

Let in the golden light,
Pull back the curtains,
Soon after the break of day.
Look through the window bright,
Push the glass and open it up,
Breathe in the early morning air.
Cold and fresh to stir your hair,
Goosebumps rise up on your skin.
Hand sweeps the sleep from your eyes,
You strain to see what the daylight brought.
Shiny sky, all hazy white,
With dappled clouds and no rain.
It will be a beautiful day.

Give it Time

Silver shone the star at night.
"You are bright," I said.
I think of you in the dark hours,
You were my help through the roughest weather.
But the storm you left me with
Was so unexpected,
I was not ready,
For such a loss.
Not by my side through life.
Tomorrow will be brighter,
Than the day before.
You said, "Go forth –
With joy to heal,
Those dark days."
"They will fly away," you said,
"Give it time."
"You were joyful once,
You can be again."
"After all," you said,
"Time is the greatest healer of them all."

Bright Sunlight

Sunlight, over bright, shimmered on the water,
Like a flash of light from a mirror.
Made me turn my head and blink,
At the enchanting rich colours of the sea.
Blue, purple, grey, green,
Soapy flecked, salty water swirling by the cliffs.
Further out, the motion of the ocean turned it to saxe blue,
Waves crashing on the rocks displayed droplets of silver threads,
Shot through with silken rainbows, one within the other.
I could see how dangerous it could be in the sea,
Undercurrents, undertow, seaweed and any amount of oil.
Seagulls bob up and down, drifting with the tide,
Some plunge down and make a sweep for something to eat,
And emerge from the depths with strangled cries.
On the horizon, a tanker glides by,
A mass of condensed water vapour floating in the sky.
The wind whistling up the cliff brings a kelp odour to breathe,
And crystals of salt to rest on the lips.
Deep breaths to fill the lungs before I potter on.

More Rain

Rain penetrated the sodden ground,
And ran into the nearest ditch.
Then flowed in a rush to the swollen river.
The storm blew itself out as dawn appeared,
Swift, shifting clouds glided along,
To show how clean the world could look.
All well-washed at the start of the day,
And the rain dripped drops from the blackberry canes.
The rosebuds dried in the wind,
Grass sparkled as the sun came up,
The blackbird and a robin sang
And the woodpecker drummed on the apple tree,
While the cat crept along the hedge.
Cobwebs were broken as he moved along
And a van splashed by in the mud.
But I felt that more rain was on the way.

Echoes of a Lost Voice

Healing will come tripping slow,
Along the pathways that can glow.
Like colours in a paintbox,
Or the encounter with a rainbow,
After an April shower.
Summer clouds sailing by,
A fleeting sight of a shooting star,
Or candlelight in a winter's night.
Moon bright, heaven sent,
Echoes of a lost voice.

And healing will come tripping slow,
Along the silver river flow,
Loosening the bonds and let us go,
Pure, simple, unpolluted.
Passing through the portal to another land,
Belief, faith or some other brand.
But understand that healing comes tripping slow.

Bewilderment and bright ideas,
Will drift about your ears.
Memories never regretted,
And the clouds will part, and the splendour
Of the heavens will open up.
And you will know,
That healing comes tripping slow.

Memories

The day after tomorrow,
Will be bright and light.
The willow by the brook,
All strands of green,
Will sway in the breeze.
With children's laughter,
A Saturday treat to fill the air,
As the swallows fly by on open wings.
Birdsong and cattle in the meadow,
Sunlight dappled on the grass,
And memories gathered of the past.
As tears trickle down out of my eyes.
The thought of you is so good,
We had such fun in the sun,
Days to remember, each and every one.
Happy, by the brook,
So many years ago.
I will not let the thought of you fade and go,
You are by the water's edge,
Where we played every summer day.
We are never apart, my sweetheart.
We are never apart.

What Next?

The tree blew down in the storm,
Plants got ripped from the soil.
The fish pond filled with mud,
Water dripped through the roof,
When the tiles crashed to the ground.
Something flew through the air,
And cracked the glass in the door.
Oh dear, and then there was a death.
To mend the mess took time,
I crawled about most morning,
On the phone, sending texts,
Not eating, never sleeping.
Days slipped into months.
Now I'm back on my feet,
Dark days are never over,
I see better, better weather.
A new tree planted; plants grounded.
Clean water in the pond.
The drip from the roof has stopped,
Fresh tiles and glass.
I'm getting in control of the grief,
Last night, I had seven hours sleep,
And I've even started eating.
Life's hard. Life's tough.
But there are good times ahead.

Pink Clouds

Pink clouds in the sky,
Drifting imperceptibly along.
The sun shifted its position,
And rays of light shone out.
Pink clouds turned orange,
Then golden in a bright blue sky.
Oh, the beauty of the clouds,
Brought tears to my eyes,
And the thought of you.
Are you up there sitting on a cloud?
Looking down on me?
The idea of you in the sky,
Comforts me.

Low Ebb

Sunlight and shadows are at my feet,
As I pad through the leafy trees.
A fresh morning fragrance fills the air,
After a night of heavy rain.
And the big fat pigeons flip, flap their wings,
As they bill and coo and nuzzle each other.
A woodpecker clings to a nearby tree,
And drums out a rhythm, one, two, three.
I'm on my own, far from the sea,
The force of water inside of me.
Gallops over the hard rocks,
Right down to the churning sea.
Out of my depth, low ebb.
I slip into a dark reality.
Slow to sigh, I could not cry.
Would the walk through the wood,
Do me any good?
I kept on walking, no more inward talking.
The storm of discontent,
Threw a veil over me, to conceal
How I feel, emotionally affected,
Inwardly unprotected, utterly defeated.
But still I go on.

Footsteps in the Snow

All week there had been a nip in the air
And many degrees of frost.
The trees and fields looked picture book clean,
Whilst I felt frozen to the bone.
And thought it too cold for snow,
But last night quite unbeknown,
Frozen flakes fell by the score.
They smothered and covered the frozen ground.
When I looked out I saw a snowscape all around,
Of a wild and wonderful land.
Frozen ice crystals one on top of the other,
Everything was so quiet, calm and still.
No fear or anxiety, serene and tranquil.
I made footsteps in the snow,
And headed for the fields I know.
Where I stopped to watch the sunrise glow,
And the beautiful snow just sparkled.
Then I followed my footsteps back home.
Alone.

Bothered

Does it bother you?
The things you failed to say.
The, "Thank you," to a teacher,
Or for the present you had last year.
Many golden opportunities,
But you let the day go by,
It wasn't until much later,
You knew what you should have said.
The letter never got written,
The phone call never made,
The text got forgotten,
As you muddled through the day.
Now, it's all too late.
They have moved a long, long way away.
But still, you want to thank them,
To this very day.
So let me say sorry.
For all the things I wanted and failed to say.

Sweet Earth

Sugared almonds and marzipan,
The sun gives us warmth and light.
For the beauty of the earth.

Fruit drops and peppermint creams,
Raindrops from the sky.
For the beauty of the earth.

Treacle toffee and creamy fudge,
The wind wakes up the trees.
For the beauty of the earth.

Dolly mixtures and chocolate drops,
Snow falls and covers the ground.
For the beauty of the earth.

Barley sugar twists and sherbet dabs,
Frost and ice break up the soil.
For the beauty of the earth.

Pear drops and aniseed balls,
Watery rivers bring new life.
For the beauty of the earth.

Lollipops and bonbons,
Things in the sea are vital for you and me.
For the beauty of the earth.

You said:
"Life is sweet."

The Phone

Navigate the waters of life
With your hand grenades held tight.
Tap the shiny, glassy screen,
Send forth the message to be seen.

Did you mean the things you said?
Now the friendship is quite dead.
It is so easy to get things wrong,
To put things right, takes so long.

Those small explosive gadgets,
Can get you into untold trouble.
You thought you were in control,
But were scammed and then defrauded.

You can wait for an answer
With bated breath, anxiously for hours and hours.
You try again but there's no answer,
'Oh! Please, pick up the phone', you cry!
I want to hear your voice one more time.

Lost

Where is the beauty of your smile?
The music of your voice?
The touch of your hand?
Why did you fade away?
Each day you slipped further away.
Your brain started to decay.
Those synapses just snip-snapped away.
I'm sorry I didn't know how to help you each day.
I didn't understand what was required of me.
I'm sorry I failed you in such a bad way.
You wept, I cried,
When the symptoms of your disease were known.
I knew long before they told us all,
About what was in store.
We were not ready for the facts,
For what was destined or intended for the storm ahead.
We struggled, confused at what we had to do.
But I, who had to watch as you stumbled on,
Could not give what you required.
And each day, I knew you would leave me.
Still, I hung on like an attendant at the gate.
But you are on the fellside now.
And I am still walking, walking on.

Another Day Dawning

Treasures of the deep
Are not for us to keep.
The dolphins need to leap.
And the corals need to grow, not sleep.

The trees need moisture in the air
And sunshine for the leaves to grow.
With nutrients from the earth,
For blossoms, seed time and harvest.

Flowers in the garden beds,
Are fragrant and well fed.
Ready to pick for a floral display,
Or left for a wonderful, pleasant sight.

The boats on the river,
Float down to the sea.
Day trippers, or fishermen and dippers.
All kinds of water birds we see.

Who will reduce the growth of plastic waste?
Use it one day and then chuck it away.
Unlike the discarded apple core,
It will not rot away.

The evening dew falls in the cool night air,
The glistening beads are everywhere.
Rain in the morning, visible drops,
Is it acid water to poison the crops?

Did you ever hear the dawn chorus?
Many birds singing at the break of the day.
That's another thing missing.
And who else has gone away?

The Greedy Sea

We never thought it would happen,
Our houses gobbled up by the sea.
They called it erosion, but I felt frozen,
As each day, my home crumbled into the foaming water.

Once my home was at the other end of town,
My neighbour's dwellings went first.
And my abode got nearer the ocean,
Where will I shelter when it has gone?

They say, "Move out; it is not safe!"
But where can I go?
They can't even provide me with a flat,
Will I have to stay in a tavern or sleep in a tent?

No compensation for erosion,
My kitchen cracked from wall to ceiling.
The wardrobe waltzed across the room,
And rain dripped in through the roof.

I will have to leave tomorrow with a sack on my back,
And my clothes in a repository and possessions in a box.
The furniture will be lost, for there is nowhere for it to go.
The lawn disappeared last week.

Now, my house is right at the edge of the coastal border,
It is so sad to see my house topple over the sandy ledge.
No one could pick up my sweet home where I was born,
And place it somewhere safe and sound.

The waves of the tide flow along the coast,
Roller after roller sweeps up the beach.
The sea surges past for more buildings to dislodge,
In bad weather, the salty air spreads everywhere.

The loudness of the pounding, swelling waves,
Is an indication that nothing can be saved.
I am like a bird with nowhere to roost.
The ransom I must pay is the house …

… where I can no longer stay.

I Spy with My Little Eye

I will raise my arms to Heaven,
And wave to you, my friend.
My life was changed just by your voice,
So don't stray too far away from me.
Sit upon a cloud and drop your raindrops,
Shining bright.
To show that you still live,
When darkness hides your face.
Pull back the veil and see my smile.
Touch hearts.
There are so many to heal.
I am reaching out to you, my friend,
As the silent clouds drift by.

Miles Away

Sitting out on the lawn,
A book and a drink for comfort.
The sun is bright and warm,
The days go by so slowly.
Without you, I'm so torn.
I feel so down and lonely,
A year ago, last spring.
You left to live in Australia,
I see you often on my screen.
We talk, but it's not the same,
As your image is in front of me.
It's not the same as being near,
I want you sitting on the lawn with me.
Close enough to touch and laugh with me.
I want you every day with me.
I'm so sorry you moved so far from me.
Don't stay away, come back to me.
Please come back to me.

Little White Feather

Feed your heart and soul
With love and kindness,
And lots more besides.
Spiritual thought,
A space inside,
Fill it with bubbles of zesty interest.
Raise your voice, you will be heard,
A perfumed breeze from the sea,
A pain inside like the ocean wide,
Purple flowers on the clifftop,
Where we walked the dog or had a jog.
Reflections in the water,
Was it you and me together?
Or thoughts of long ago
When we were young.
Your heart my soul,
Together we swayed,
Twisted like a three-strand rope.
You, me and one other.
The other was our spirit,
Transient, lasting but a moment,
But we were together,
Ephemeral, effervescent, fleeting,
Like a fugitive passing by.
What was felt was not expressed,
Silent soul, silent heart,
Whispers in the dark.
And I found a little white feather.

Take Time

A time to grieve,
Time to say goodbye.
Today, tomorrow,
A place no one can share.
The dreams we had
Will fade away.
Did you know that time
Can stretch a long, long way?
Time for this and time for that,
But no time for grief.
Bereavement, sorrow or sadness,
Sunshine will take time to come back.

A Prayer

Dear Heavenly Father,
I have a deep need for your support.
May your beautiful, wonderful light
Shine down on me,
Your sad, sad servant.
Hold me in your hand,
Awaken my spirit,
To feel your majestic help.
Feed my soul with hope,
Enfold me in your arms,
Comfort me every night,
Stay close by my side.
Touch my heart,
Let sorrow flee away.
Brighten my empty day,
I earnestly ask for your assistance,
And thank you for your help.
Amen.
Amen.

Night-time Treasure in the Heavens

The scarf around my heart,
Wrapped to keep me warm.
The fleece of woven wool,
Shone with a sparkle of dewdrops bright.
I had been out all night,
Watching the moon roam across the sky,
Wondering what magic it would provide.
The power of blended love,
Followed stars as they shot across,
The sooty arch above,
As unseen angels voices reached me.
Oh, the sweet, perfumed air,
Intoxicated my insides.
I would see from that time on
Only love was born.

Beauty and Wonder of the Spirit

Snowdrops, daffodils, delightful Spring flowers,
Be sensitive to physical effects of every kind.
Try to understand the other side of depressing,
Glorious, entrancing of wondrous powers.
Listen to your inner mystic,
Clutch hold and let it rip,
Let the tip of the iceberg melt,
Never feel guilty for feeling great.
Step into your power,
The beauty and wonder of the spirit.
Mix together, ultramarine and lemon yellow,
And get green.
Music makes you happy, sad or glad,
The beauty and wonder of the spirit
Will transport you to a happy place.
Travel on, travel on to a spectacular space,
Espy with your inner eye,
A wealth of valuable memories.
And what's in store; look forward to more,
Beauty and the wonder of the spirit.

Helping Hand

Why did you have to go away?
The sky is so dark and grey
It feels like a Winter's day.
Ice, snow and rain,
Stays with me and won't go today.
Who is going to give me a helping hand – I am.
Who is going to be there when no one understands – I am.
When someone tells me things I don't want to hear,
Who is about to give me a listening ear – I am.
When the day is dull and I am sad,
Who is ready to grab my hand?
I am – The Lord.

Soulmate

You were the coal to my fire,
The wood to my flame.
The heat to my heart,
The match to my spark.
Kindled love in my heart
Still brightly burning,
No tears will extinguish the glow.
A fragile breeze remains,
To wrap me up and keep me warm,
And watch the ember's luminous light,
Stay another night.

Pending

I will know when I have to let you go,
Are you down below or up above?
There's things I need to tell you,
I know you're in a garden not far away.
Those splinters from the woodwork are still irritating me,
And the clothes you used to wear
Have been neatly folded away.
Your photos are on the bookcase,
I look at you every day.
And I eat the food that you used to like,
But still, I hate the taste.
Is there really a place called Heaven?
Or are you somewhere else?
Your friends don't know what to say to me
So, they just stay away.
I listen to your music
But it gives me little joy.
And I will spread you where you said,
"We must be nearer God in this particular spot."
But I can't put you to rest,
No, not yet.

I Love You Long and Dearly

The bell tolls
And I get no sleep.

I washed my slippers
So, my feet will be clean,
To walk the celestial way.

The pen that needs to write
"I love you long and dearly."

And I prepare to wait
For our next meeting.

The bottle of wine
Is still in the fridge.
Ready, ready for drinking.

What time is it?

The little harvest mouse,
Ran up the dandelion clock,
To see what time it was.
He huffed and puffed,
But the parachute seeds did not move.
"What time is it?" his fellow mice cried up to him.
"Time will not go backwards,
And time will not go forwards,
We are free," he said.
"It's free time."
And all the mice went home to live another day.

Silver Chain

We were locked together with a silver chain
Even when you were far away.
The chain remained,
We never thought a link would break.
But it did.
Like popcorn, it just flew apart
And I never saw you again.
Whilst something heavy fell into my heart,
It was cold, big and rough.
I carried it around for a week and a day,
What was the hefty thing I would say,
That had fallen right into my heart.
The weight was great,
Was it a stone or some other kind of rock?
Why was this thing so dense and hard?
I asked a question and an answer I required.
I sat and pondered and listened a while,
Then the pain and sorrow began to flow out,
The cold, hard stone started to melt.
The lump of salt came out as tears,
And I know that the silver chain
Was still linked to me in a special way.
And you jumped right into the space
Where the heavy thing had been,
And you will forever be linked in me.

A Murmuration of Starlings

The birds came in; I saw them all arrive,
Their bodies are green with a purple sheen.
Starlings, they gathered on the tall pylon posts
A splendid sight as they prepared for flight.
They took off en-masse at evening time,
All turned in a moment like a big black shadow of light.
Birds all swirling together in wonderful formation,
With absolutely no smashing, crashing together.
They twisted and turned, swept low to the ground,
Then up to heaven in a beautiful cloud.
To cry out a blessing,
Brought near by a breeze.
Could every black bird represent someone in need?
They were all together to let me know,
Their murmuration was a spectacular show.
While silent harps played within my heart,
An act of commemoration of love and trust,
The birds in flight a jet-black mist.
I saw them circle, climb and glide,
Like a crazy blanket in the sky.
Unending, changing, turning, they took my breath away.
And so, the flock gathered in size,
A hundred more and more besides,
Thousands stretched their wings out wide
Never a collision, never a collide,
They swooped and swirled from side to side,
Telling me I would survive.
The heartache, the sadness I felt inside,
How could so many birds come to my aid?
Such a stupendous sight of impressive birds in flight,
Then, they all fell to the ground for a good night's sleep.

Pursue Tomorrow

Better days, better days will greet you,
One fine and clear morning.
No longer the bitter taste upon your tongue.
Trees have started to leaf,
Flowers have begun,
The day is warmer than the day before,
And there will be things you want to do.
Clean and scrub and make all things new.
You feel like going out,
To meet your dear friends,
Who have been waiting at your door.
They will be there to say 'hello',
And talk to you once more.
So that laughter can flow through you,
To say welcome to the new dawn.
Lots to look forward to, lots of things to do,
You will feel happy once more,
A fine day to start you on your way.
Keep going, no more sorrow,
You have lots to look forward to,
Tomorrow.

The Essence of the Sea

The wind blew my skirt about my legs,
I licked my lips like a lolly on a stick,
Salt crystals on my tongue and round my mouth.
The taste was so good I did it again.
Green, blue, oxygenated sea,
Lapped smoothly on the yellow ochre sand.
The effervescent fizz as the waves trundled in,
Caressing the ground with such a gentle hand.
I strolled along the water's edge and wet my painted toes.
The bottom of my feet got sandpapered down,
Cool, refreshing runnels swirled around my heels.
Shrimps were swimming in the shallows,
Broken shells and seaweed fronds,
Were scattered along the sandy shore,
Left high and dry as the tide had turned.
The seagulls shrieked as they swooped on by,
And spreading their wings, flew back around.
The smell of the sea made me feel quite free.
And I went wild and danced up the beach.
Then, after the rains, the butterflies came.

The following pages contain poems which include references to suicide, abuse, stillbirth and child loss. The author has chosen to include these as true representations of reality because these experiences are also major sources of grief. Though they fit the premise of this book, some readers may find this content difficult and/or upsetting, particularly if directly affected by these issues. Please, therefore, exercise caution when reading.

I Wept (for my child)

My child, my child,
All stiff and cold.
My child, my child,
You came, we loved, you left.
My child, my child,
I am bereft.
My child, my child,
There is nothing left.
My child, my child,
I'm glad you stayed awhile.
My child,
Chained to my heart.
My child,
Chained to my heart.
My CHILD.

Miscarriage

I miscarried on the twenty-eighth of September,
I remember it as clear as day.
I had a belly rumble,
And it turned into a terrible pain.
I lost my Sophie or Robert,
I didn't know which it would be.
I grieved for my dear foetus,
For the baby I never knew.
They would never go to school.
I wanted to watch my baby grow,
But instead, I had to go to bed,
And let my child go.
I cried a lot for days and days,
Until I could cry no more.
I wish I had known,
Whether it was a girl or a boy.

Teardrops (for my child)

The flame of my child
Burned bright.
I thought you would live,
But a breath of wind
Came and smothered the light.

Dear loved, beloved,
My child is dead.
And the ache is worse than
The birth.

The night is dark
And I cannot see.
Silent nights.
Tender moments, float free.

To the Abused, Bereaved

Those insults etched their way into your body,
Unjust words coiled up inside.

You thought the bad feeling would go away,
When they were not here anymore, anymore.

Absorbing so much over the years,
You're broken down and ill at ease.
They caused you so much trouble,
For years and years and years,
And you can't shed a tear.

The abuse they gave so freely,
Pulled you down to the ground.
Now you feel quite alone, still fermenting inside.

But the torment and hurt still go on and on.
So please, put your hurt into a box,
And seal it down and throw it out to sea.
Let it float upon the tide, away to the other side,
Never to be seen again.

No more unkind words to haunt you,
You thought you would be fine now that they have gone.
But the pain you felt at their disdain.
Will take time to drain away.
Melt away like ice in a drink,
Truly, it will take time to heal.

Take shelter under the umbrella
Of self-love, compassion and self-respect.
You will slip from the dark into the light.

Gather up the hateful words in your mind,
And put them in a boat and send,
Them off for an ocean trip,
Never to be seen again.

Now you have time to heal.

Little by little, you will say, "I am different now,"

"I can have a future without – You."

Beyond Grief

They said suicide, suicide, did they?
They said suicide; I don't remember.
They came, they said, they went.
Sheer shock.
Why did I not know?
Was there a cry for help?
Oh, my dear one,
Why, oh why?
You hid your hurt so well,
I did not know you had such pain,
The letter you left tried to explain.
Terrific guilt, so sorry I failed you.
You said you were struggling and had help in the past,
This time, you hid it so well.
I did not realise you were in trouble again.
You had an illness that led to death;
Your mental health.
When did the enemy get in?
Robbed of so much; you, me, us.
Beyond grief.
Where are you now?
Somewhere I cannot see you.
Suicide, suicide.
It stretches you into eternity.
What next, oh dear me.
Life flies by like a dandelion clock,
We didn't have time to stop, make a wish
And enjoy the moment.
The seeds at the top blew away before they should.

If only I had taken time,
To notice what was right there before my eyes.
A person so sad at life,
Who could not function anymore.
The following days, I felt ripped quite raw.
Overwhelmed, adrenalin pumping,
Alone with myself, dragged under a bus.
It took time to come out the other side,
And to know that I must love myself.
To accept the body I have to take me through life.
Some things which happen are beyond my control.
I think that the company I choose to keep
Is so critical to my well-being.
Suicide.
That word chills me to the bone.
As I weep into my hands.
A life lost before its time.

The Swans (a traumatic death)

Two swans flew over my way,
Their necks outstretched, so solid and strong.
Big wings flapped lazily on.
As they circled round,
And then flew low,
Down to the water far below.
How happy I was to see them go.
Mates for life, I'm told.

Oh! What happened to them next?
Someone said that a pellet from a gun,
Had shot one through the neck.
I cried for that bird, the poor bird who died,
Shot with a pellet from a gun.
The swan's mate stayed with its friend,
That should have been paired for life.
Instead, one lay dead.
Shot with a pellet from a gun.

Who thought it fun to end its life?
A week later, I saw a swan fly over,
On its own, with its neck outstretched,
So solid and strong.
Its big wings beat the air, lazy and forlorn,
I hope it finds a safe place and a new mate.
To start life again …

… in a new place.

♥♥♥♥♥

May calm slip in beside you and hold your hand as it guides you through your raging sorrow.

Go steady, let the hurt dissipate, the trembling slowly evaporate and there be no more whispers in your head.

Reinvent those tender qualities instead.

Wild Woman sends her kindest regards to all of her readers.

A place for my thoughts ...

A place for my thoughts ...

A place for my thoughts ...

A place for my thoughts ...

A place for my thoughts ...

www.ingramcontent.com/pod-product-compliance
Lightning Source LLC
Chambersburg PA
CBHW041147110526
44590CB00027B/4157